LATE HARVEST

LATE HARVEST

A Collection of Later Year Poems

Miriam Laserson Varon

Matador
9 Priory Business Park
Wistow Road
Kibworth Beauchamp
Leicester LE8 0RX, UK
Tel: (+44) 116 279 2299
Fax: (+44) 116 279 2277
Email: books@troubador.co.uk
Web: www.troubador.co.uk/matador

ISBN 978 1780880 402

British Library Cataloguing in Publication Data.
A catalogue record for this book is available from the British Library.

Typeset in 12pt Book Antiqua by Troubador Publishing Ltd, Leicester, UK

Matador is an imprint of Troubador Publishing Ltd

For Lenny and Dani

And with gratitude to a true friend, Cathy Moritz

PART I

LEGACY

I went for *Yahrzeit* to the place
where my father's ashes are buried
so far from where he lived – so far
from when he lived.
My memories
are an inverted telescope
in an unsteady hand.

I have so far
inhabited this life
thirty years longer
than the length
of all your days.
I thank you
for your share in my being here
and place a small stone
next to your name.

ODE TO MY LEFT ARM

You always played second fiddle,
separate and inseparable,
until your strings were torn
when on a hilly sunlit country road
a wheel detached from a decrepit truck
that plunged into and almost took
two lives.
When on the seesaw between here and there
they told me I might have to let you go,
the threat became a challenge:
I held on to you and you
hung on to me
and we went on together.
Throughout the years
my injured forelimbs have combined
whatever they had left in strength and range
to carry out the multitude of tasks
imposed on human hands –
lift loads, shell peas, write poems, cradle babies –
and when my right arm faltered
after years of service,
you took over.

So here I am,
balanced between
my gallant limbs,
all wounded veterans of life.

LISTENING

Perhaps I do not hear so well
but I do listen
tuned in
to sound – and silence –
open to
the voices on the wind.

AGAIN

I will again climb
a mountain.
I will.
I will put one foot
a little ahead of the other
and shift my weight
forward,
upward.
I will again rise
to meet the wind
on the heights
that answer my yearning.

INSIDE-OUT

What if clothes were worn
with all the stitches showing
and smooth inside –
What if the injuries
inflicted on the soul
were filtered out
to leave us
at peace
inside.

STILL
(Written on Still Street, Brookline)

Has winter come?
Not quite –
some roses
are still in bloom
and I can look
into the sun
by blinking
just a little;

a very quiet voice
– one not attached
to any words
one that vibrates
without a sound –
bids me to trust
the wisdom
of the seasons.

8

THE DISTANCE

When we were new arrivals
in each other's life
you told me
you had traveled
at so fast a pace
that fate
did not owe you –
whatever lay ahead
would be a bonus
you were eager
to spend with me.
And so
we have roamed
across frontiers
and time
on unpaved roads;
we do not know
the distance still to go
nor can we divine
– a knowledge I would dread –
which one will be ahead
across the finish line.

*Postscriptum:
you have gone
and I must find a way
to forge ahead,
complete the course
as best I can.

9

THE TWINS

Never and forever –
inseparable twins
unborn
unbearable
unconceived
and inconceivable.

BIRTHDAY

Four score and ten
the number
of rings around my life
their markings
blended
as they are crushed
into an intersecting trail,
the destination undisclosed;
the weight
is mine to bear,
the journey
mine to travel
and the alloted span
mine to accept.

ROSES OF SEPTEMBER

I paid a visit
to the roses
of September
late bloomers
and survivors
among the tired
wilting heads
that add
their dab of color
to the masterpiece.
We who can hope
to greet the blossoms
of another spring
are the custodians
of your beauty.

AT SEA

I am cruising time
tossed about by gusts
frightened, elated
doubtful of my course
sensing the depths
and never certain
am I passenger
or navigator.

DISORIENTATION

No
I am not losing
my mind
my mind
is losing me
soaring to heights
and sliding
into depths
so steep
so deep
I cannot follow
cannot reach
the steering wheel
nor would I know
which way to turn

A LIFE

A life
cannot be measured
by the space it fills
nor by the time
it stays afloat
upon the shoreless sea.
A life
is not a garment
turned inside out
for longer wear.
It cannot be returned
nor must it be discarded.
There is no borrowing,
no lending,
no exchange,
there is no way
to try it on.
One to a customer
and every single one
bespoke.

LEAVING THE PARTY

I shrug a chip of rancor
off my shoulder
and slip some disappointment
down my sleeve
the last log has begun to smolder,
the lights are dimming – time to leave.

THE STREAM OF TIME

The stream of time
does not flow smoothly
from untraceable source
to a mouth beyond reach
the waters may seem
stagnant or swift
as they proceed
on their inexorable course
conveyer belt
of the inanimate
the one-way mobile home
of every living creature
the battlefield
for the lone swimmer
against the current:
memory.

A WALK

I held your hand
to steer you
through the perils
of a walk.
We passed
a building site
"look Mama"
you said
"the crane is gone."
Close to half a century
has passed
and we are clambering
across the rocks
that line
another continent,
another sea
Here – take my hand
and steer me
through the perils
of a walk.

THE MILL

The sun is low
behind the hill
a distant glow
the rays no longer burn
the trail is winding
to skirt an ancient mill
the wheels no longer turn
and still
I hear them grinding.

THE TIDES

So many waves
have slammed
against this shore
so many
have touched
with a caress
and gently
pulled away
in the unfathomable
mating dance
of land and sea
I stand
upon this earth,
my native soil
and face the sea
with Love and Fear,
my twins,
that have refused
to separate
and often
do not allow me
to recognize
which one
I cradle.

THE UNBORN

The words
I failed to herd
into a poem
are children
I did not bear
to term.

THE FLUME

In this flume
the walls close in
too tightly
to be navigated
by echo-sound
it is too dark
to spot a crevice
wide enough
for passage
the stepping stones
are far apart
too far
to serve as ladder
toward the rim.

PILGRIMAGE

I am at home in exile
I do not know from where.
So many forks and crossroads
chosen – I know not how.

My pace has slowed – not so
the turbulence of choice.
And still I do not know
Whence and whereto and why.

TSUNAMI

Oh, the desolation
of empty graves
of love unburied
roaming
through the void
in search of shelter
no peace in life
or death
until eternity
has shrunk
into a womb.
When you feel
the reach of a tsunami
for your bed in the ocean
fear is swallowed
along with hope.
You have become
the eye of the storm.

WHITHER

There are the highways
with speed limits and access roads
and there are streets
with names and homes
and there are trails:
trails on which you walk
whether you can or cannot tell
where they will lead.
Each step a child
of your own strength,
your own sense of direction.
The end of any drive
is destination –
the road to destiny
a solitary walk.

Pas de deux

GEMINI

Alate
and elated
on the wings
of changing winds

I am a Gemini.

My mind weighs and accepts –
my heart is violent.
I do not love with teaspoons.
Yes, my mind
measures the cataract and knows its depth
and yet – I leap.

I must be swept into the whirling fall,
engulfed and pounded by the maelstrom's force
unto my very core
and then emerge
in clear, cool waters;
in my blood
the deep serenity that comes
to woman after birthing
Or be devoured.
So be it.

Sometimes I ask myself:
how would it be
to meet my mirror-self –

the one
whose heart is tranquil
and whose mind
is passionate.

Twin of my envy, blessing and desire –
Where are you
and how do you fare?

GEMINI – THE OTHER TWIN

My mirror-self
twin of my envy and desire
I have outlived you
as you dwell in me.

I have stepped into places
you left open
I ceded you the room
I did not need.
And yet as turbulence
has rocked my mind
I never wholly felt my heart
at peace.

Imbued with the explosive mixture
of waning vigor
and of waxing reach
I stride and stumble
between doubts and wonder
toward the mystery
of a conclusion.

THE DUST I RAISE

The dust I raise
is a reminder
of long forgotten steps
along the way.
The distances of living
are not from here to there –
space has no dimension
in a life
that flows
from now to then
time
leaves no traces
has no point of origin
no destination.
Whoever says:
I have no time
or:
I have time
offends
the very notion
of the word.

THE HARDEST OF WINTERS

The fallow time of the mind
is the hardest of winters.
The wells of spring
are frozen;
only the touch of a warm hand
raises the fuzzy image
of what seemed
the boundless surge
of the flame.

ANOTHER SPRING

Another spring –
what have I sown
what flowering
will bear the traces
of a soul
in turmoil
and a mind
that rides the range
no reins, no saddle
nothing but the storm.

NEILAH

This congregation
of young people
has the freshness
of a mountain tarn
that ripples in the wind.
The waters are drawn
to the outlet
and replaced
by the incoming waves.
Except for an occasional
lined face –
a friend, a relative –
only the rabbi and I
have grown older
year by year.
He stands at the center,
the fountain that lifts
and dispenses the waters.
When I am called
to let the spray
rise through my voice
I am happy.

TASHLICH

Every year
on *Tashlich*
I throw bread
into the flowing stream
to unburden the spirit –
let go
of the ballast
that makes me navigate
in murky waters.

In the course of the year
every crumb
will have turned
into nourishment
and I pray that the spirit
will go on to ride
whatever comes
down the river.

ON THE MARCH

Young voices
are meant to rise
in exultation
above the tread
of the crowd.
But whenever
disdain
stifles the voice
of the old
a guardian angel
leaves.

NO GLASSES

Memory – the eye
that scans the past –
as we grow older
the far-away is clear
the view up close a blur.

IN THE RING

I am thrust
into a wrestling match
I did not seek
do not enjoy
and cannot win.
Still – I prefer
to enter into the ring
rather than watch
the fight.

MT. AUBURN

Here in the cemetery
where my past is buried
I breathe solace,
free the vents
clogged by regrets,
inhale the presence
of waterlilies and dragonflies.
In the rippled mirror of the pond
the nightmare shapes of doubts and pains
reflect as shadows of the clouds.

MY NAME

Sometimes I feel
that I no longer fit
into my name;
I have long outgrown
the one I shaped
with the tongue of childhood
when I still lived with those
who called me so.
Then there were years
away from home
when I resided
within my given name;
the time was right
the place was right
I was the one
called thus.
It is no longer so.
I can't say when it was
that I began to feel
a stranger in my name –
neither do I know the right one.
Mama, Mom,
And Grandma
are sounds of bliss
that anchor me

within the web
that is my life –
until the day
when my name
will be written
in stone.

THE PATHS I WALK

The paths I walk
are shorter
and not as steep
as those
on which my memories
are climbing
to breathless heights –
I listen
to the distant echo
of a waterfall
and hear the roaring
of a raging river
a gentle breeze
evokes
the mighty storms
that threatened
long ago.

THE PATH TO SIGNAL HILL

I walk
slightly behind you
as we ascend
to Signal Hill
along the narrow
rocky path
that skirts the cliff;
here I can breathe
the air within my body
descends and rises
with the wind
returning
the joy of living
to the sky above.

GOOD DAYS

Some days
are good days
without tears
and then there are
good days
because you cry.

THE TARN

Could I
cry words
instead of tears,
a cataract of poems
would descend
these rocky cliffs
and gather
in some enchanted
hidden tarn.

THE CLIMB

A pen or pencil,
a scrap of paper –
they are my limbs
for climbing
out of an abyss
onto a mountain
each word a step,
each line a rope,
and when I reach the top
the view as unpredictable
as the completed poem.

SUPPRESSION

My fingers close around a pen
my mind refuses to divulge
the words to tame
the storms
within.

A POEM

Written on sand
and blown into
oblivion;
written on water
and swept out to sea;
a stream, a trickle
from arcane
breeding grounds,
condensed
into the disembodied
chalice
of a poem.

THE SHROUDS

Naked rage
or despair
born in silence
destroy their womb;
words are shrouds,
muting ministers
to the bare violence
in the soul.

MINDQUAKES

The capillaries of the brain
scrape rock
the mind stumbles
along the unfamiliar paths
the signposts have been scattered
place is nowhere
time has no dimension
smiles and sighs
laughter and screams
attach themselves at random
to incongruous feelings
and the dust devils of things past
are swept
from one corner to another.
Mindquakes
do not give birth
to volcanoes.

THE RIDE

We creatures of this earth
are spun at random
on our ever turning carousel.
At random our turn is over
and we are flung into the void.
We do not know
how many turns we'll take
before the music stops;
we do not choose
our neighbors nor our rides.
We buy a ticket –
and we wave
and smile
in passing.

A WAVE

The old,
the feeble,
the impaired,
walk with a cane –
of their four limbs
three labor
for each step;
one solitary hand
remains at liberty
to reach, to touch,
to wave
to someone
across the street.

THE JOURNEY

This journey through a life
is made atop a cart
pulled by a team
unmatched
in strength, in speed
and in endurance;
the signs along the way
are written
in a language
we do not understand;
smooth pavement
alternates
with stretches
of unpaved road;
goal and duration
are kept a mystery
until the ride
has ended.

PART II

THE CAVE ARTIST (ALTAMIRA)

In the vault above
a dance of giant shadows
is called
by a tiny flame
that struggles
in a crevice of rock.
Supine
on a bed of rock
I raise my eyes
I raise my hand
holding a piece of rock
and pray
for the prey
whose image emerges
conjured by the encounter
of hand and rock.
The globule of color
traces the path of my arm
the strength of the bison
enters my fingers
and the herd above
sweeps me
into the unknown to come.

PANEGYRIC

I'm fit as a fiddle I'm told
perhaps – like a fiddle of old –
Amati and Strad are my sisters
the veneer shows some blisters
some dents and scratches
and off-color patches
but the touch of a bow
makes me vibrate and glow
and raise my choice of sound
to praise beauty unbound.

THE OLD WATCH

The hand that showed
each minute going by
has slowed;
You dear old face –
it seems you try
to match my pace.

THE ROLLER COASTER OF OLD AGE

The roller coaster of old age
is steep
and frightening –
the riders not inclined
to underscore
their thrills and fears
with screams.
They lean back in their seats
and watch;
the music fades
the wheels touch down
on level ground;
the time has come
to disembark.

THE GAZEBO

Serenity –
even the hummingbirds
suspend their frantic flutter
clasp the perch
in a moment of rest;
two ducks
move quietly
on the small pond;
the surrounding trees
drip sparkles onto the soft ripples
of the green mirror
where the flowering bushes
create a tremor of color.
The picture is perfect;
suddenly
in the lower right corner
appears a chipmunk –
the signature of the artist.

THE CHIPMUNK

I watch a chipmunk
looking for a place
to hide a meal
against the days of snow.
I am in awe of you
my nimble friend –
when you will need
your buried treasure
you will know where
to dig.

PAEAN TO A TREE

How dare I write
a paean to a tree
on paper –
a distant relative
has fallen to provide
this flimsy surface
for the vain attempt
to paint in words
your flaming crown
of glory.

A few days hence
a cataract
of fiery hues
upon the path
will turn each step
into the sacrilege
of treading
royal ground.

When all along the street
the skeletons of trees
recruits in gray
present their arms,
you will be known
by your position only –
the one that holds
the corner.

And then
there will be days
when ermine
bedecks your limbs
in homage
to your majesty.

THE SHELTER

I entered
the golden splendor
of a thread-leaf maple;
I was at home
in an enchanted castle,
the open-air cocoon
of branches
embraced me,
gave me room to move
and made me feel
a welcome guest.
When it was time to leave
I knew my mind had found
a place I could repair to
whenever I had need
of shelter.

IN THE DEEP

I let myself be carried by the flow
to move among the creatures of the reef
and I was awed
by being suddenly endowed
with freedom I had never known.
The fish were birds in flight
and so was I
released into a new dimension
no wings, no fins
and yet allowed
to share the ecstasy.

THE CORRIDOR

A train – a window seat –
the body is at rest;
all but the hand that holds
onto the straps
of pad and pencil,
while the mind
is swaying,
moving with the train
along a track
of ever-changing vistas,
a blending
of seasons, motives,
landscapes of the mind,
a many-layered aggregate
linking the here and there,
the now and then.

JOY

There is no fine
and no award
for joy
no shape, no aim
joy may enter
in an explosion
or surreptitiously
and may or may not leave
a trace of passage
an embroidery
a giggle.

IN THE LIBRARY

My intramural refuge:
a cubicle – an empty shelf,
an inkstained desk –
the hum of silence
set in parentheses
of steps,
a child's raised voice,
a creaking chair.
In this grove
the foliage is compressed
in walls of books
divisions
between divergent emanations
of thoughts in search of words.

FLOW

I wish I could
dispatch a message
of admiration
to my kin:
artesian wells
that never cease
to overflow
and never
run dry.

THE BLUE DRAGONFLY

There was a flutter
dancing on my sleeve
a whiff of motion
time enough to feel
the tug that joins
all creatures.
That instant
an invisible
indestructible stitch
was added
to the web of life.

VISITOR

I feel the shadow
of a touch
upon my hand.
A dragonfly
has landed.
I have never seen
the likes of it:
the body cherry-red
across the wings
black sprinkles
enhance
a net of gossamer
that catches
the primal glow
of beauty.

JUNE

A sunny afternoon
is reaching
into the open chalice
of the senses.
They merge
and shed
their separate
realms.
June
is the time
of joining.

AT THE RESERVOIR

With wedgelike wakes
in glinting circles
the ducks, performance artists of the pond,
draw their ripple design in the water,
while on the other side
a flotilla of geese
in tight formation
presents a precise
naval maneuver.

ROSES AND TODDLERS
(Minot Rosegarden)

Helmeted warriors
race tricycles,
their pounding knees
decorated
with bandaids.
Three little girls resolve
the dilemma of a threesome
with a triple hug.
A very gentle breeze
lends a slight sway
to the stems of roses.
The shadows of the trees grow longer
and the line of daredevils
on top of the slide shorter.
The children's voices fade
and the birds take over.

TREES IN FLOWER

Pink and white
bridesmaids of the spring –
hope and fulfillment twinned
on tree arms
that reach out
in prayer and praise
I want to hang
the raggedy shreds
of my thoughts
my pains and joys
on these easels
of the divine artist
the creator
who called beauty
into being.

FIRST DAYS OF OCTOBER

I did not plan to come
but here I am
the sun is warm
some of the roses
still in bloom
the noise of cars
no more than counterpoint
to chirping on the wing.
I will go home in a while;
the fragrance
of sun and roses
will last me
through the night.

A PLACE BY THE LAKE

I have come home
to this place
where nothing is mine
nothing
can be taken
the ten measures of beauty
have met here
to hold their sway
over this moment
bird cries escape
a coil of silence
spread
across the water
the lake hides
some of its splendor
beneath
the reflected darkness
of the woods.

*For Aaron (translation of German poem by Miriam Laserson
dated January 1, 1943)*

WELCOME TO THE NEW YEAR

Poor little mite, be not in fear
of all those strangers, those grim creatures
with their exhausted, cruel features:
the veteran days of the departed year.

Pay them no heed – be on your way
you have your eyes to steer you right
and no one can avoid the plight
of resolutions gone astray.

You never know – let come what may –
let fortune have a chance to smile;
a whiff of peace – a lovely day –
enough to make your trip worthwhile.

You newborn year, be free, be bold,
bestow new faith, dispense new power,
discard the shackles of the old
and, pray, make our garden flower.

INSPIRATION

In awe and hope
I reach
into man's treasure:
the cornucopia of words
that holds
the flow of chatter,
curse and blessing,
the elusive gems
of wisdom,
the frayed edges
of silence,
the vault
of the unsaid.
I reach – and pray.
There is no poem
of virgin birth.

THE SAILOR

Words are
the element of man
and I have sailed
the seven seas
in stormy weather
or becalmed
slicing through waves
that rose up to engulf
my tiny craft
or hovering
between the threat and pull
of alien shores.
I am where I belong
the wind my chart,
the sea my home.

CURRENCY

The voice that speaks
provides the entrance fee
into the human race;
the spoken word,
the touchstone of entitlement,
embraces
a multifaceted array
of need and want,
of rank and privilege,
of range and ken.
We are what we can say.
We are what has been said to us.
The power of the spoken word
is all embracing, though it be held
deliberately in abeyance.
The words not said
are our ramparts,
The words we speak
are our currency
as members
of humanity.

SOUND

Sound
a birthday present
to the world
the building blocks
for noise – and poems –
invisible collisions
engender
the currency required
to connect
the solitary seeds
of silence
before creation.

PART III

PONDERINGS

Season of beauty, season of strength

Patches of last week's snow
glitter in the sun
flecked
with a scattering of leaves
drained of all colors but brown.
Brown touched by the sun
into a many hued palette
that merges
with the crowns of the trees:
the pared-down crowns.
The pale blue of the cloudless sky
creates
a designer network of spaces
between the bare branches,
a magic transition
from the splendor of the living tree
to the stark beauty of the skeleton.

* * * * *

A sun-touched bench among the trees
the bare embroidery of twigs and branches

filters the glowing message of our star
unto the snowy patches on the ground,
while on the ice-bound inlet of the nearby pond
blazes a ball of fire.

* * * * *

An empty nest
suspended
in the bare branches
of a wintry tree:
a touching witness
to the promise of the seasons –
an apostle of hope.

* * * * *

Here is my pen, my hand,
my brain, my heart
here is the moment
here my prayer
and the happiness
of feeling held
like a pen –
of being moved.

* * * * *

Each passage through this world advances
in random sprints of vigor and dismay;
dimensions change
shapes disappear
and a flicker of sunlight
reflects in a mirage.

* * * * *

A little while ago, when I took up my pen,
there were words in me
to open a passage through the night,
a reflection of the starry sky
in the mirages of St. Elmo's fires –
it was a passage opened for a prayer
to rise and merge
with the flicker of the stars.
I do not know
how to catch a flicker
and translate it
but I feel
the touch, the meaning
of what escapes
understanding.

* * * * *

One day I was sitting on a bench
in the small garden near the pond
I lifted my closed eyes
into the sun
a flood of light
penetrated through my lids

the stream of time
in a rainbow of color
a flood of happiness.
I wrote it all down
for my children and grandchildren
in better words than these
and the piece of paper disappeared. Still
I want to pass on the message.

* * * * *

Displacement
the flip side
of freedom
5 days outside – what?
A palisade,
a web of barbed wire,
both prison and safety net?
Now that I am back,
I feel
not confined,
but disoriented.
Burdens have a way
of shaping
into anchors.

* * * * *

My daily prayer
is a walk
around a pond
I do not claim
to walk with God
but as I walk
I feel a blessing
walk with me.

* * * * *

I stumble and I feel
a hand that stems my fall
a moment added
to my count of blessings.

* * * * *

A sultry afternoon
I see the ghosts
of last month's violets
scattered among the grass.
And then a squirrel
scampers across
and scatters the illusion.

* * * * *

The world of the mind
is an impenetrable coil
that cannot be unraveled
without being destroyed.
All the world's writings
are fallout from the writhings.

* * * * *

A rope of many knots
lies coiled
in a forgotten corner
of the soul –
a random pull
raises the snake.

* * * * *

On this bench
the mind lets go of the words
to meet the birds and the trees
on their own terms.
In the indoor park
of the library
I look around me
and in one moment of looking
I take in hundreds of minds
in millions of hours
to catch words; their shape
their meaning
their connection,
and combine them
into sentences and paragraphs.
The force that creates this process,
the energy that propels it,
what is it?
Where is it
when it is not perceived?

* * * * *

A hidden bullfrog sends
a raucous signal of his presence
across the pond
and soon a deeper rumble
returns the challenge
across the water.

* * * * *

Among a stand of somber trees
A gleam of golden bronze
draws my attention
and then I see:
a withered leaf
emblazoned
by a ray of sun.

* * * * *

Language – a stream
that gushes forth
from the sea of the mind
and returns to feed it.
Every language has its speed,
its temperature and taste
and a mission.

* * * * *

When my prayer
rises among the trees

I know it goes
in the right direction;
roots spread
sap rises
and wings unfold.

* * * * *

The smell of wet earth
pervades
my perception.
I recognize
the smell of wet earth;
perhaps it perfumed
the birthing fluids
when I entered this world.

* * * * *

Solitude within the pressure of the outside:
opening up without being assaulted
breathing in and breathing out
without swallowing or expelling poison
the challenge of living
on this earth.

* * * * *

Knowledge is a giant
that swallows its own scions
and excretes
information.

* * * * *

Memories –
so much to remember
so much to forget.
Some memories reach out
with great persistence,
some pounce to maul you,
some play hide and seek
and keep you guessing
whether they are
a spider's web of moments
distilled
by your imagination
out of the random tides of life.

* * * * *

As my range is shrinking
I need more strength
to reach beyond
and more wisdom
to choose
where and why.

* * * * *

I do not wish to use
philosophy and poetry
as a screen
to hide
from the floods and storms
that devastate
the world.
Words and thoughts
are prayers
spoken and unspoken,
signals sent
into the unknown;
it is the sending that matters,
whether or not
they be answered,
whether or not
we would recognize
an answer.

* * * * *

There is an echo in my consciousness
of sounds I cannot hear
a song I cannot sing
the echo fills
the hollows of perception,
makes them impenetrable
to the voice of reason.

* * * * *

I raise my glass
to celebrate
the victory of grape
over gripe
of wine
over whine
and I salute
the daughters of Noah.

* * * * *

A flight of words
propelled into the void
a flimsy web
across a raging stream
moving is peril
standing still, perdition.

* * * * *

Return to the womb
yearning for shelter
the place of being
before becoming
absolute peace
in the absence of choice –
does seed have
a homing instinct?

* * * * *

* * * * *

I have to keep reminding myself
that this is late September;
I am sitting here
enjoying the sun and the roses
both are nourishing me.
I cannot think of the right word,
but I can feel it with all my being.
I close my lids – the light is overwhelming.
When I look again
the tips of the petals
on the tallest
of the roses
are still glowing.

* * * * *

The most powerful telescopes
of earth's observatories
explore the features of the stars,
pull them
within our ken.
The wonder of the universe
is reflected
in the eyes of an old woman
sitting on a bench
in the park.

L